MEDIEVAL BRITAIN

The Medieval Church

Peter Chrisp

Titles in this series:
Life in Medieval Britain
Medieval Monarchs
The Medieval Church
The Norman Conquest

Cover: Two monks praying.
Title page: Monks sing the holy services in the choir of their church.

Series editor:
Geraldine Purcell
Book editor:
Carron Brown
Series and book designer:
Simon Borrough
Book consultant:
Dr Matthew Strickland

© Copyright 1996 Wayland Publishers Ltd

First published in 1996 by
Wayland Publishers Ltd, 61 Western Road,
Hove, East Sussex BN3 1JD

British Library Cataloguing in Publication Data
Chrisp, Peter
The Medieval Church - (Medieval Britain)
1. Great Britain - Church history –
1066–1485 – Juvenile literature
274.1'05
ISBN 07502 17464

Typeset by Simon Borrough
Printed and bound by G. Canale & C.S.p.A.,
Turin, Italy

Picture acknowledgements
The publishers gratefully acknowledge the permission of the following to use their pictures in this book: Lesley & Roy Adkins 26; Bridgeman Art Library, London/British Library, London 8, 15, 19, 20, 31, 44, /Church of St. Michael, Diddiscombsleigh, Devon 18, /Fitzwilliam Museum, University of Cambridge 25, /Lambeth Palace Library 10, /Toller Fratum Church, Dorset 13, /Trinity College, Cambridge 24, /Church of St. Mary, Kidlington, Oxfordshire 44; C. M. Dixon 5 (bottom), 23; Sonia Halliday Photographs 12, 29, 38, /F. C. Birch 33; /Laura Lushington Photographs *cover*, 4, 5 (top), 6/7, 35; Topham Picture Source 36/37; Wayland Picture Library *title page*, 17, 41, /British Library 42.

All artwork is by Barbara Loftus.

Contents

Jesus Christ

In the Middle Ages (AD 500-1500), most Europeans were Christians, followers of the religion started almost 2,000 years ago by a Jew called Jesus. Jesus lived in Palestine, which was ruled by the Romans at the time. After preaching for less than 2 years, Jesus was killed in AD 32 by being nailed to a wooden cross. This was a Roman punishment used for foreign rebels.

Christians believed that Jesus was God himself, the maker of everything. They said that God had chosen to be born as a human being and to die on the cross. Jesus had then shown that he was God by rising from the dead three days later.

The idea of God coming to earth and becoming human was seen as the most important event in the whole of history. It was so important that we still date years from the birth of Jesus Christ. 'AD' or 'Anno Domini' means 'the year of the Lord', and 'BC' stands for 'before Christ'.

The baby Jesus, held by his mother, is given presents by three kings. This was part of one of the many stories that Christians told about the founder of their religion.

The world as a battlefield

Christians saw the world as a battlefield, in which the forces of good fought against the forces of evil. On the good side, led by Jesus Christ, there were the angels and the saints. Angels were beautiful beings with wings like swans, created by God before he made humans. Many Christians believed that they had their own guardian angels watching over them, defending them from evil and suggesting good thoughts.

Saints were human beings who had lived perfect Christian lives and had been granted great powers by God. The most important saint of all was Mary, the human mother of Jesus Christ, who was called the 'Queen of Heaven' and 'Our Lady'.

Every Christian had his or her part to play in the battle against evil, through prayer and good deeds.

The forces of evil

The forces of evil were a host of devils led by Satan, who is more commonly called the devil today. Once they had been angels, but they rebelled against God and were thrown out of heaven. They became hideously ugly; their swans' wings turned into the wings of bats. Christians believed that these devils were everywhere, stirring up trouble and trying to lead people astray. These devils wanted to capture the most important parts of men, women and children, called souls.

Above *A carved angel flies through the air, playing a harp.*

Below *Satan, in the centre, and his army of ugly devils torture the damned in hell.*

Hell was described in the 1050s by a churchman called John of Fécamp:

'There is nothing there beyond a river of fire and a foul swamp. Angry devils live there with arms like the heads of dragons, their eyes shooting out fiery arrows, their teeth sticking out like the tusks of elephants.... There is always the sound of wailing and weeping, groans and bellowing ... There is no rest for the sufferers.'

The after-life

Christians believed that when their bodies died their souls would carry on living in an after-life.

Hell

The souls of the wicked – those who had been led astray by the devil and his host of demons – would be sent to hell to suffer in agony for ever.

Heaven

Christian souls that had been saved went to heaven, to live with God and the angels. Heaven was said to be a place of perfect happiness and rest, sometimes described as a garden filled with beautiful scents and wonderful music. The joys of the saved were increased because they could look down on the sufferings of the damned in hell. They could then be thankful to God that their souls had been saved and taken up to heaven.

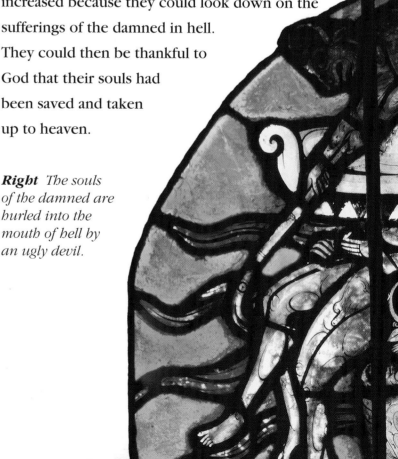

Right *The souls of the damned are hurled into the mouth of hell by an ugly devil.*

Purgatory

From the twelfth century, the Church taught that there was a third place where people went after death, called purgatory. Like hell, this was a place of suffering; but it was also a place of hope. People in purgatory were there to burn away all the sins from their souls. Only then would they be worthy to enter the gates of heaven.

Most Christians would have to go to purgatory before being allowed to enter heaven; only saints went straight to heaven. Christians believed that the time the dead suffered in purgatory could be shortened through prayers and special church services, called masses. Rich people always left money in their wills to pay for masses to be said for them after they had died.

The Last Judgement

Christians believed that their bodies would rise from their graves on the day that the world came to an end. In those last days, there would be terrible disasters - rainstorms of blood would fall from the sky, the stars would drop to earth and the sun would turn black. After these events, an angel would appear in the sky and blow a loud blast on a trumpet. At this signal, all the dead would climb out of their graves to be judged by Christ. This would be the day of the Last Judgement.

Throughout the Middle Ages, many people believed that this terrifying Day of Judgement could come at any time.

This artist imagined the Church as a tower under attack by heretics. Defending the tower you can see a king (near the top of the tower), two nuns (praying at the windows), four bishops (in tall white hats), two cardinals (dressed in red) and the pope, on the right, who embraces the tower.

The word 'church' means 'belonging to the Lord'. In the Middle Ages, the word had more than one meaning. In the broadest sense, it meant the body of all good Christians. It included those already in purgatory and heaven, together with those on earth who would one day be saved. The Christians on earth belonged to the 'Church Militant' (fighting), because they were still struggling with the devil. The dead Christians belonged to the 'Church Triumphant' (victorious), because they had won their own battles over the devil.

The word 'church' also stood for the organization of full-time church people called the clergy. These were people, such as priests, monks, nuns and friars, who had promised to spend their lives in the service of God. People who did not belong to the clergy were called the 'laity'.

The Catholic Church

In the Middle Ages, there was only one official Church in Western Europe which was known as the Catholic, or 'all-embracing', Church. The Catholic Church was well organized. Each country in Western Europe was divided up into large areas called dioceses, each headed by a powerful churchman called a bishop. The bishop had his headquarters in a large church called a cathedral. In turn, each diocese was divided into small regions called parishes, each with its own small church and priest.

Heretics

The Catholic Church claimed to know the only way to reach heaven. Christians who disagreed with Catholic teaching were called heretics. The Catholics believed that heretics had been led astray by the devil. Their ideas had to be stamped out. Heretics were more dangerous than unbelievers, because they were more likely to lead other Christians away from the true path to heaven.

In the 1390s, a religious writer called Walter Hilton wrote of heretics:

'A heretic ... takes delight in clinging to his own opinion, holding it to be true, although it is contrary to God and Holy Church ... But he deceives himself, for God and Holy Church are in such unity that whoever opposes one opposes both ... Indeed, unless God in His mercy sends him humility while he lives, he will in the end go to hell. Yet he thinks that he has done well, and that he will win the joys of heaven.'

> 'The pope can be judged by
> no-one; the Roman Church has
> never made a mistake and never
> will until the end of time; the pope
> alone can depose and restore
> bishops; all princes should kiss
> his feet.'

The head of the Church in Western Europe was
the bishop of Rome, also called the pope, or
father. In the early Middle Ages, the pope was not
very powerful. At that time, the kings and queens
acted as the real heads of their Churches and they
chose their own bishops. But after 1050, the pope
began to claim more and more powers.

*An English king kneels
before the pope, kissing his
ring as a sign of respect
and obedience. The men
dressed in red are
important Church officials
called cardinals. They
chose each pope from
among their own number.*

King John and Pope Innocent III

The pope's new powers were resisted by some kings. One of the worst quarrels was between King John of England and Pope Innocent III. In 1208, King John refused to accept an archbishop of Canterbury appointed by the pope. Innocent reacted by closing the churches of England. For six years there were no church services – no masses, weddings or funerals. King John was excommunicated. This meant that he was denied the protection of the Church, and all Christians were forbidden to have anything to do with him.

It was a difficult time for the people of England, because they had to learn to cope without the comfort and services of the Church. With no holy protection from the Church, it seemed to many of the people of England that the devil was being given a free hand to cause trouble.

In 1213, John backed down and accepted the pope's archbishop.

The quarrel shows just how powerful the pope had become. King John never tried to keep the churches open on his own authority. Even while quarrelling with him, King John accepted that the pope was the true head of the Church.

King John has the worst-recorded reputation of any English ruler, partly because he quarrelled with the Church, and it was the monks who wrote history in those days. After King John's death, one monk summed up John: *'Foul as Hell is, it is made fouler by the presence of John'.*

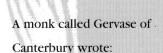

A monk called Gervase of Canterbury wrote:

'Great sorrow and anxiety spread throughout the country. Neither Good Friday nor Easter Sunday could be celebrated, but an unheard of silence was forced on all the clergy and monks ... The bodies of the dead, whether of the ordinary folk or the religious, could not be buried in consecrated (holy) places ...'

The church was the centre of village life. It was the place where everyone gathered at least once a week, on Sunday, to worship God and swap news. The church was the tallest building in the village and often the only one built of stone. Its walls were covered with religious paintings, especially paintings of the Last Judgement, showing the damned being dragged to hell, and the saved climbing to heaven. These were the only pictures that most people ever saw and they believed that what they saw was true. This encouraged the villagers to become good Christians so that their souls would be saved. The images of hell terrified the people into worshipping God.

Churches were divided into two parts. The holiest area was the eastern end, called the chancel. This was where the altar (a table with a large cross standing on it) was placed. It was here that the priest recited the services, which were in Latin. The western end of the church, called the nave, was for the ordinary worshippers.

The priest

Only men could be priests. Apart from leading the services, a priest was meant to explain Christian beliefs to the ordinary people. He taught them how to say prayers and, if he was a good priest, preached to them about the life of Christ.

The village church of Hardham in Sussex, its walls covered with religious paintings. In the Middle Ages there were no seats – the worshippers stood in the nave, the large area in the foreground. In the background you can see the chancel, the holy area where the priest said the services.

Holy water

Holy water, which was water blessed by the priest, was kept in the font, a stone basin used for baptizing babies (see page 17). The holy water was thought to have the power to keep evil spirits away. On entering the church, people dipped their fingers into another basin of holy water kept by the door, making a sign of the cross.

The priest had an assistant, whose job was to carry the holy water around the parish. People sprinkled the holy water on their homes, animals and food.

Tithes

The maintenance of the church was paid for by a tax called a tithe, or tenth. All the villagers had to pay a tenth of their income. Usually this meant a tenth of the crops they grew in the fields. If people did not pay, the Church had the power to arrest and punish them. They could also be arrested for other offences, including heresy, witchcraft, eating meat on a Friday, or failing to go to church. Punishments included beatings, fines, imprisonment and excommunication.

The font was often covered with religious carvings. This carving, from Toller Fratum Church, Dorset, shows Christ's death on the cross, between two thieves.

Blessings and curses

The priest had the power to bless and to curse. There were special blessings to protect houses, cattle, crops, wells, the sick, and people setting off to travel. Curses were used against heretics and devils, and used to drive away caterpillars and other pests from crops, and kill weeds.

The people had their own prayers in English to say during mass. This is one prayer:

> *'Jesu, lord, welcome thou be*
> *In form of bread as I thee see.*
> *Jesu, for thy holy name*
> *Shield me today from sin*
> *and shame.'*

The mass

The priest's most important role was to say mass every day. This was the service where a small wafer of bread and a cup of wine were thought to change into the body and blood of Christ. Only a priest had the power to perform this daily miracle.

Almost everyone went to mass on Sunday, and some began each day with the service. People described going to mass as going to see God, their maker. When they looked at the holy bread, they felt that they were seeing Christ.

During mass, the priest wore special robes and recited a long Latin service, accompanied by various gestures, such as signs of the cross. To the worshippers in the church, it seemed like a magic spellin in which everything had to be done correctly. The priest stood with his back to the ordinary worshippers. Most of them could not understand the Latin words that he was saying.

The most important moment of the ceremony was the elevation, or lifting, of the holy bread. While bells were rung, the priest raised the holy bread above his head so that the kneeling people could see it. Villagers working in the fields nearby could hear the bell being rung. By kneeling and facing the church in prayer, they could share in the benefits of the service.

The priest then ate the bread and drank the wine. Not a drop could be wasted. If a fly had fallen into the cup, it had to be swallowed too.

Sometimes, the bread was reserved, or saved for

This picture shows a mass said in a nunnery. While nuns ring bells, the priest says mass in front of the bread, which has turned into Jesus Christ. You can see Christ in the top right corner.

later use, such as being taken to the sick. It was kept locked in a beautiful silver or gold container, called a pyx. From 1311, on the festival of Corpus Christi (the Body of Christ), the bread was carried in its pyx on processions in every town in Britain. Pyxes were even carried into battle.

The service of mass was thought to bring many different benefits. There were masses for the dead to help their souls leave purgatory and reach heaven. In wartime, masses were said to protect the king and the country. There were even masses to bring good weather.

Taking communion

In the 1440s, a churchman called William Lyndwood wrote a set of instructions for priests on giving communion. The most important instruction was that the holy bread, Christ's body, should be treated with great respect:

'They should not break it up with their teeth, but should swallow it down as little broken as possible, lest any small part of it remain between their teeth or elsewhere.'

Despite this, there were stories of people hiding the bread rather than swallowing it, and carrying it away for other uses. The holy bread was thought to have great magical powers – it was worn as a charm against bad luck, and ground up and sprinkled over the garden to keep caterpillars and other pests away.

As time went by, many people began to go to confession and communion at other times of the year, such as at Christmas. By the end of the Middle Ages, some Christians were eating the holy bread once a month.

Communion, confession and penance

The sight of the holy bread being elevated by the priest was thought to bring great benefits to ordinary Christians. Some religious townspeople rushed from church to church, in order to see as many elevations as possible. However, the greatest benefit of all came from eating the bread. This was called taking communion, or being houselled. Christians were expected to take communion at least once a year, on Easter Sunday.

In order to be worthy to eat Christ's body, people had to be in as pure a state as possible. First, they had to confess their sins to the priest. People usually confessed at the beginning of Lent (see page 20), during the week called Shrove-tide, meaning 'the time of confession'.

The priest then gave people penances to do in order to wipe out a sin. A penance might be saying a set number of prayers, fasting on bread and water, or going on a pilgrimage. Serious sins brought tougher penances. In the 1050s, one English nobleman, Swein Godwinson, was ordered to walk barefoot to Jerusalem as a penance for a murder. Swein reached Jerusalem, but died on his return journey.

From birth to death

The Church had a special ceremony to mark each important stage in human life. New-born babies were welcomed into the Church by being baptized. The dying were helped into the next world by a priest saying the last rites.

Baptism

During baptism, the priest poured holy water from the font in his church on to the baby's head, saying three times, in Latin: *'I baptize thee in the name of the Father and the Son and the Holy Spirit'*. The child was then given a name, anointed (rubbed on the head with holy oil) and marked with a sign of the cross.

Christians believed that they were not complete until they had been baptized, and that an unbaptized baby could not go to heaven if it died. Baptism was also thought to drive out any devils that might be possessing the baby's body. The devil's were forced to flee the church by the north door, sometimes called 'the devil's door'.

A new baby is baptized over the church font. The priest stands on the right.

Confirmation

The next ceremony after baptism was called confirmation, designed to give children extra power against the devil. Confirmation had to be done by a bishop and so it was also known as 'bishopping'.
The bishop placed his hand over the child's head and made a sign of the cross. Most bishops had little time for this duty. Some bishops confirmed children from horseback while riding from one village to another.

Marriage

Marriage was performed in a churchyard or in the doorway of a church, and the couple were then led inside for a mass.

Last rites

The dying were visited by the priest, who heard their confessions and gave them communion. This was called the *viaticum*, or provision for the journey (into the after-life). In the Middle Ages, it was common to see a priest rushing to visit a sick person, carrying the holy bread, covered by a veil. His assistant went before him,

This church window shows the holy bread being offered to a dying man as part of the last rites. The priest's assistant, on the right, carries the pyx in which the bread has been kept.

ringing a bell and carrying a lamp, so that passers-by would realize that Christ's body was being carried among them. The on-lookers were expected to kneel and pray.

Burial

All Christians wanted to be buried in a churchyard, in holy ground close to a church where the masses could help them get to heaven. The churchyard was also a good place to be at the Last Judgement, when all the graves would open and the dead would climb out.

The priest says the funeral service, sprinkling holy water on the dead body, which is wrapped in a white sheet called a shroud. In the background, an angel holds back a devil with a cross, helping the soul of the dead person fly up to God.

Christianity gave shape to the year through its religious calendar. There were four big festivals: Advent, Christmas, Lent and Easter. Each festival marked an important event in the life of Christ. There were also many saints' days, when different saints were remembered. These church festivals and saints' days were much more familiar to ordinary people than the days of the month. People said 'St Michael's day' or 'Michaelmas', rather than 29 September.

Advent was the festival preparing for the coming of Christ. Christmas celebrated his birth. Lent marked the forty days he was said to have spent in the desert, fasting. Holy Week, at the end of Lent, re-enacted the events leading up to his death on the cross. Easter was the great celebration marking his

Bishops were powerful and important men. Yet they were sometimes made fun of, even during holy days. This entertainer with a performing dog is dressed as a bishop.

resurrection, or rising from the dead. This was followed by Eastertide, the forty days that Christ was thought to have spent on earth after rising from the dead. By celebrating these festivals, Christians re-enacted Christ's life in a great yearly drama.

The festivals matched the different seasons. Lent, the time of fasting, took place in late winter, when fresh food was most scarce. Easter, the resurrection, saw the arrival of Spring bringing new life. It seemed as though the whole of nature was working to the rhythm of Christianity.

Holy days

Sundays and Church festivals were called holy days. On these days most work stopped. The Church hoped that people would spend their free time in Christian worship. In practice, however, most people went to mass and then spent the rest of the day having fun. So through holy days lies the origin of today's word 'holiday'.

Lent and Easter

For each of the big festivals, there were impressive church ceremonies. On 'Ash Wednesday,' at the start of Lent, the priest blessed ashes and scattered them on the heads of the people, warning them that they were *'dust, and unto dust they would return'*. At the same time, all the crosses in the church were covered up with white cloths. A white curtain was also spread across the chancel, hiding the holiest area – the high altar – from the nave.

Fast days

Fasting was an important part of Christian life. Christians believed that there was a constant battle between their spirits, or religious sides, and the demands of their bodies for food, comfort and pleasure. By denying their bodies' demands, people believed that they could free their spirits.

On fast days, people were forbidden to eat any animal products except fish. Meat, milk, butter, cheese and animal fat were all banned. The number of meals was also limited. Apart from the big fast, Lent, there were many single fast days on the eve of great festivals. People were also forbidden to eat meat on Fridays and Saturdays, though they could eat as much as they liked of other foods.

The yew tree

Beside every church in the Middle Ages there would be at least one yew tree planted in the churchyard. These trees were very special to the people because they symbolized immortality (life that lasts forever). This was because the yew tree is a type of tree called an evergreen, which means that it stays green all year round, never dropping all its leaves like most other trees. For this reason, the twigs of the yew were used during the Holy Week to represent the immortal life offered to good Christians by God.

Holy Week

Lent ended with 'Holy Week', when the events leading up to Christ's death were re-enacted. Palm Sunday, at the beginning of the week, celebrated Christ's entry into the holy city of Jerusalem. In the Bible, the people of Jerusalem welcome Christ by spreading palm leaves in front of him. So the Church marked this by blessing and handing out palms to the people. These palms were twigs of yew, a tree planted in every churchyard.

Carrying their palms, the people walked in a procession around the churchyard. On their return to the church, the priest threw back the curtain hiding the chancel. At the sight of the great cross, everyone knelt and shouted three times, *'Ave Rex Noster!'* ('Hail our king!').

Maundy Thursday

On Maundy (Commandment) Thursday, thirteen poor people had their feet washed by the most important people attending the church service. This marked the event of Christ washing the feet of his own followers during the Last Supper.

Good Friday

The day after Maundy Thursday was Good Friday, the day of Christ's death. People crept on their knees to the cross and worshipped it. The host, the holy bread, was placed in a stone or wooden tomb, called an Easter Sepulchre.

Holy Saturday

Holy Saturday was the time of waiting for Christ to rise from the dead. In the late afternoon, the people stood in the church, in darkness. Meanwhile, outside, a new fire was lit, struck from a flint. A candle, lit from the fire, was then brought into the church. This was to show that Christ was on his way back from the dead.

Easter Sunday

Easter Sunday was the day of great celebration, when Christ was welcomed back to life. At the first light of dawn, people went to church to see the holy bread, Christ's body, being solemnly lifted out of its tomb. Then everyone received communion.

A woman confesses her sins to the priest in order to receive communion, something that everyone did at the beginning of Lent.

Monks

Monks were men who chose to live apart from the everyday world, in monasteries. When men became monks, they had to make vows, or promises. They promised to give up all their personal property, never to marry and always to obey their abbot, the chief monk.

The monks' way of life was laid down in a rule, a set of instructions drawn up by the founder of their order. The most famous rule was written by St Benedict in the sixth century. His followers were called Benedictines.

The monks' most important task was to sing the Divine Service, a collection of Bible songs praising God. They had to do this seven times every day and once in the middle of the night. This was called the 'work of God'. The monks spent the rest of the day in study, prayer and in work in the fields of the monastery.

St Benedict's aim was to teach the monks to be humble, to realize how unimportant they were compared with God. This was why they spent so many hours each day praising him. Being obedient, working

Monks had an important role writing and copying books by hand, and decorating them with beautiful pictures. Many of the pictures in this book were painted by monks.

in the fields and having no possessions of their own, helped the monks to be humble. For the same reason, the monks all dressed alike in simple black robes called habits.

A bishop meets a group of nuns, led by their abbess (the chief nun).

Nuns

Women could also choose to live apart from the everyday world, by becoming nuns. However, there were far fewer nuns than monks, for they mostly came from rich families. Nuns had paid servants to work in the fields for them and their rules were less hard. Nuns were often widows, or daughters for whom husbands could not be found. Several English queens became nuns.

Monks and nuns lived the religious life for its own sake. Even so, people believed that their services helped everyone in the battle against the devil.

A royal document founding a new monastery at Winchester in AD 966 explained the benefits of the monks' work:

'The abbot is armed with spiritual weapons and supported by a troop of monks ... They fight together in the strength of Christ with the sword of the spirit against the aery wiles of the devils. They defend the king and clergy of the realm from the attacks of invisible enemies.'

Life in a monastery

Monasteries were important for the whole neighbourhood. These religious communities were great landowners, providing work for local people in their fields. Monasteries were like hotels, offering shelter and food for travellers. Many ran schools for local children and gave alms to the poor – daily gifts of food and clothing, to beggars who waited at the gates. They grew herbs for medicine and treated the sick. Monasteries were also places where books were written and copied, and where the great works of ancient literature were preserved.

Fountains Abbey

Fountains Abbey, in Yorkshire, was founded in 1132 by the Cistercian monks. They were an order who followed a stricter rule than the Benedictines. The Cistercians liked to settle in remote places in the countryside and live as simply as possible.

There were two groups of people living at Fountains Abbey. There were the monks, who concentrated on singing the services in the choir of the church. There were also lay brothers, who were men who wanted to follow a religious life but who were less well-educated than the monks. It was the lay brothers' job to do most of the farming work. They chopped down trees and looked after the sheep in the surrounding fields.

The monks and the lay brothers lived in separate parts of the monastery. Near the bottom of the plan, on the right, you can see the frater, or dining room, of the lay brothers. Above it is the frater of the monks. Each group had its own dorter (sleeping area) and infirmary too. An infirmary was like a hospital and an old people's home, where the old and sick brothers were looked after.

The chapter house, next to the church, was the building where the monks met each day to discuss important business. Alongside

This photograph shows the holiest part of Fountains Abbey, the eastern end of the great church, where mass was said each day in front of nine altars.

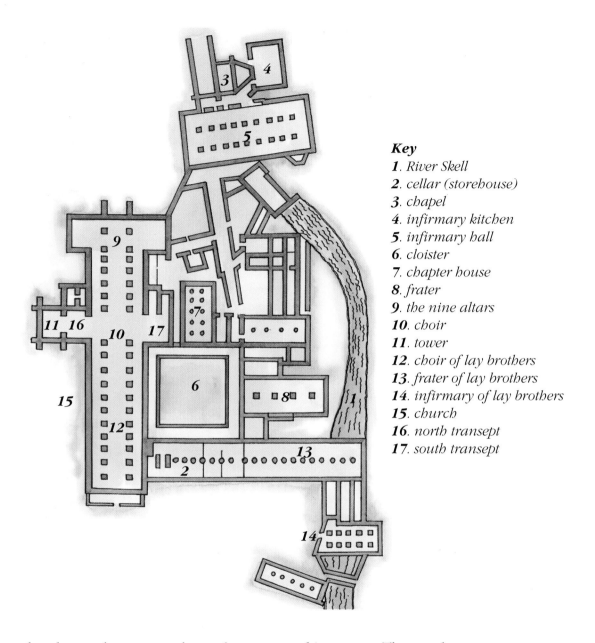

Key

1. River Skell
2. cellar (storehouse)
3. chapel
4. infirmary kitchen
5. infirmary hall
6. cloister
7. chapter house
8. frater
9. the nine altars
10. choir
11. tower
12. choir of lay brothers
13. frater of lay brothers
14. infirmary of lay brothers
15. church
16. north transept
17. south transept

the chapter house was the parlour, or speaking room. The monks were usually supposed to keep silent, except for prayers and official business, and the parlour was the one place where they could chat.

Apart from the church, the most important part of the monastery was the cloister – the square, covered walkway that linked the different buildings. When they were not in church, the monks spent most of their time here, walking, studying or writing.

This is a plan of Fountains Abbey by the River Skell in Yorkshire.

In the early 1200s, a new kind of religious order appeared. Its members were called friars, or brothers. Unlike monks, who shut themselves away from the world, friars were men who went out among the people to spread the Christian faith by preaching. Another big difference was that, while monks worked for a living, the friars relied on gifts. They were called mendicants, or beggars.

The Franciscans and the Dominicans

To begin with, there were two main orders of friars: the Franciscans, or grey friars, founded by St Francis; and the Dominicans, or black friars, founded by St Dominic. At first, there were big differences between them: St Dominic's aim was to fight heresy through preaching; St Francis was more concerned with living as simple a way of life as possible, teaching by example. But, in time, the orders came to resemble each other closely.

Matthew Paris, a monk living at St Albans, described the arrival of the Franciscans in England in the 1220s:

'Dwelling by tens or by sevens in cities and towns, owning nothing whatever, living according to the gospel, preferring the utmost poverty in food and clothing, walking barefoot, they showed the greatest example of humility to all men.'

The friars as scholars

By the late 1200s, there were around 100 British friaries (friars' houses), mostly in the bigger towns. Here, friars were trained to be expert preachers, to hold an audience's attention through story-telling. Friars also became university teachers, at Oxford and Cambridge. Through study, they hoped to work out the best ways to convert the whole world to Christianity. As a result, the greatest European scholars of the Middle Ages were friars.

Like priests, friars were given the right to hear confession. Since they were better educated than most priests, the pope believed that they would be better at giving religious advice to ordinary believers.

The friars were so successful that their orders grew very rich on the gifts they received. As they grew wealthier, many people began to accuse them of forgetting their original aims. Fourteenth-century English writings are full of complaints about the greed and easy life of the friars.

The poet, John Gower, wrote of friars:

'The friars preach of poverty, yet they always have an open hand to receive riches ... They wish ease, but they will not labour. In no case do they do their duty.'

29

For some Christians, the life of a monk or a nun did not go far enough. They chose to cut themselves off even more completely from the world, by living alone, and worshipping god as hermits or as anchorites.

Hermits

Hermits lived in lonely places, such as forests or caves, spending their days in fasting and prayer, battling with the devil. *The Life of St Guthlac*, a story about an English hermit, describes the sort of battle that was thought to take place:

'He suddenly saw the whole tiny cell filled with horrible troops of foul spirits ... They were ferocious in appearance ... with great heads, long necks, thin faces, yellow complexions, filthy beards, shaggy ears ... Leading him away, they plunged him into the muddy waters of the black marsh ... they took whips like iron and began to beat him ... they began to drag him through the cloudy stretches of the freezing skies to the sound of the horrid beating of their wings.'

Anchorites

Women rarely became hermits. They were more likely to be anchorites, people who chose to be walled up for life in a small cell, often attached to a church. Many towns had several of them. Their prayers were thought to help the whole town in the battle against the devil.

Unlike monks, who had a whole community helping them lead a religious life, hermits had only their own resources to rely on.

The *Rule of St Benedict* describes hermits as the front-line troops of the Church:

'Hermits ... after long training in a monastery, having learnt together with many brethren how to fight against Satan, go out well-armed from the ranks of the community to the solitary combat of the desert.'

Guthlac edificat fibi capellam.

St Guthlac, a famous hermit, builds a chapel – a place where he can be alone and pray. A chapel was for private worship, unlike a church, which was for everyone.

Punishing the body

Hermits and anchorites put themselves through all kinds of physical discomfort. They wore itchy clothing made from animal hair; they recited their prayers while sitting in a tub of cold water; and they flogged themselves with knotted ropes. Like fasting, these were all ways of punishing the body to free the spirit.

Nobody thought that there was anything strange in living like this. The hermits and anchorites were admired for living a life so completely devoted to God. People often went to ask their local anchorite for religious advice, speaking through a small window in the wall of the cell.

The biggest buildings of the Middle Ages were the cathedrals, the great churches where the bishops had their thrones (cathedrae). There were two types of cathedral. Some, such as Winchester and Norwich, were also the churches of monasteries. The services were sung by monks who lived in the neighbouring buildings. Other cathedrals, such as York, Wells and Exeter, were not part of monasteries. In these, the services were sung by canons, ordinary churchmen who lived in the town.

A cathedral was cross-shaped and, like a parish church, pointed east, towards the rising sun. The eastern end contained the bishop's throne, the high altar for mass and the choir, where the monks or canons sang the services. The western end was the nave, the huge hall where the worshippers stood or knelt. Apart from stone benches around the walls, for the old and sick, there were no seats in a medieval nave.

Cathedrals were built to be as imposing and beautiful as possible, both to honour God and to

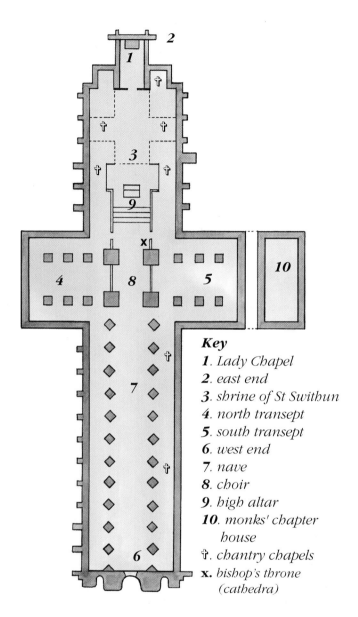

Key
1. Lady Chapel
2. east end
3. shrine of St Swithun
4. north transept
5. south transept
6. west end
7. nave
8. choir
9. high altar
10. monks' chapter house
✝. chantry chapels
x. bishop's throne (cathedra)

This is a plan of Winchester Cathedral.

impress the ordinary worshippers with his power. At a time when most buildings were small and made of wood, the very sight of a cathedral was awe-inspiring. For a worshipper standing in the nave, looking up at the carved angels on the high ceiling and listening to the singing from the choir, it was like getting a glimpse of heaven.

Holy days

On Sundays and Church festivals the nave was used for colourful processions. To the music of trumpets and organs, the monks or canons walked slowly around the nave and into the choir, carrying banners and crosses. At Norwich Cathedral, on special festivals, a carved angel was swung from the ceiling of the nave, waving perfumed smoke over the heads of the worshippers.

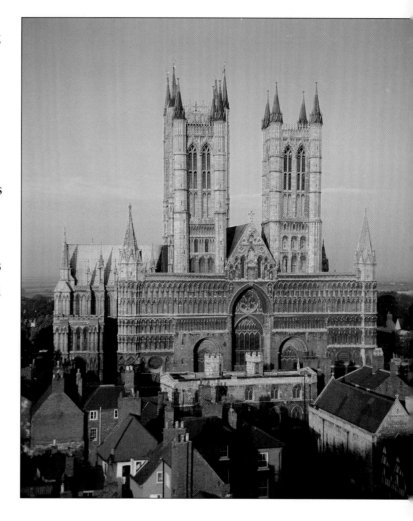

Lincoln Cathedral towers over Lincoln town and the surrounding countryside.

Chapels

Around the sides of each cathedral, there were a number of small chapels – places for private worship. Some chapels were devoted to particular saints, and there was usually a 'Lady Chapel', for the Virgin Mary, at the far eastern end. There were also small chantry chapels, built by the wealthy to help them get to heaven. The wealthy left money in their wills to pay a priest to chant, or say, a mass for their souls there, at least once a day.

Relics

All cathedrals owned holy relics, such as saints' bones or bits of wood, believed to have come from the cross on which Christ died. These were the most prized objects in the Middle Ages, and churchmen went to great lengths to get hold of them. In the twelfth century, Bishop Hugh of Lincoln, was visiting the town of Fécamp in France, which claimed to have the body of St Mary Magdalen. While the local monks watched in horror, Bishop Hugh chewed off part of St Mary's arm-bone to take away with him!

The most important relic in a cathedral was usually the skeleton of a saint, kept in a large stone shrine. At Durham Cathedral, there was the shrine of

St Cuthbert; at Winchester Cathedral there was the shrine of St Swithun; and Canterbury Cathedral had the shrine of St Thomas Becket.

Pilgrimages

People went on pilgrimages to visit these shrines. There were many different reasons for going on a pilgrimage. For some people it was a penance; others went to ask a favour of the saint or to thank the saint for help in the past. A pilgrimage was also a good excuse for a holiday.

For pilgrims, visiting the shrines was like going to see the saints themselves. The saints were thought of as powerful living presences with their own personalities. St Cuthbert, for example, was known to have disliked women, and so only men were allowed to approach his shrine. Durham Cathedral is one of the few cathedrals without a 'Lady Chapel'. When people tried to build one, in 1140, cracks quickly appeared in its walls. This was taken as a sign that St Cuthbert did not want such a chapel built near him.

Pilgrims' guidebooks were books that described the benefits you could get from visiting the various saints. This is a twelfth-century description of the shrine of St Giles:

'One must pay a visit with particular attentiveness to the most dignified remains of the most pious and Blessed Giles ... It is he who, ahead of all other saints, is accustomed to come most quickly to the help of the needy, the afflicted and the anguished who call upon him. Oh what a beautiful and valuable labour it is to visit his tomb!'

A stained-glass window from Canterbury Cathedral shows St Dunstan – one of the three saints who had shrines in the cathedrals.

Healing shrines

A saint's body was believed to give off great power, which could enter any object placed nearby. People pressed their rings or jewels to the shrine, to capture some of this power. There were also niches (hollows) at the base of the shrine so that pilgrims could get even closer to the saint. Sick people would crawl into the niches, begging the saint to cure them.

The mentally ill were brought to shrines, often chained to stop them hurting anyone. In the Middle Ages, madness was believed to be caused by devils who had possessed, or taken over, the body of the sufferer. These devils would be driven out by the saint.

A monk or canon usually stood near the shrine ready to write down any cures in a 'book of miracles':

'A possessed boy was so violent that seven men bound him ... Taken to Norwich, as they approached the tomb he screamed 'What do you want with me? Where are you taking me? I won't go there.' Bursting his bonds he attacked his mother ... sinking his teeth into her throat. Overpowered and taken to the shrine, he was soon cured.'

Offerings to shrines

The pilgrims brought offerings with them, including coins, jewels, rings and wax candles. Sick people brought silver or wax models of the part of the body that they wished to be healed. Those setting off on sea journeys left models of ships.

People who had been healed, left the evidence behind – a kidney stone, for example, or a sneezed-up cherry stone, which someone had almost choked on, mounted in a silver box. The most common such offerings were walking sticks or crutches. The monks or canons kept all the offerings as a sign of the power of their saint.

Some offerings were an important source of money for the cathedral. Visitors to St Thomas at Canterbury provided a quarter of the cathedral's yearly income. Thanks to the wealth provided by the pilgrims, the monks were able to give their saint the most richly decorated shrine in Britain.
It was described by an Italian pilgrim:

'Despite its great size, it is all covered with plates of pure gold; yet the gold is scarcely seen from the various precious stones with which it is studded, such as sapphires, diamonds, rubies and emeralds; and wherever the eye turns, something more beautiful than the rest is observed.'

Monks carry a saint's relic in a procession. Below the relics, some people who are unable to walk are shown praying to the saint, hoping to be cured.

Christians realized that there were other religions in the world besides their own. They knew about Jews, who lived in small communities in towns throughout Europe, and Muslims, who ruled the lands to the south and east of Europe.

Muslims

Muslims were thought of as the *'enemies of God'* by Christians. They were especially hated because, for most of the Middle Ages, they ruled over Jerusalem, the holiest place in the world for Christians.

The pope launched a series of crusades, or religious wars, to seize control of the 'Holy Land'. The Church also set up crusading orders, such as the Knights Templar, whose members were like fighting monks. Christians believed that to die in battle against Muslims was one way of reaching heaven.

A crusading army gets ready to sail for the 'Holy Land' to fight against Muslims. The ships are loaded with supplies.

Jews

Christ and his earliest followers were Jews. However, most Jewish people had rejected Christ's message, and they were also blamed by Christians for his death on the cross. This was enough to make them the *'enemies of God'*, like the Muslims, in Christian eyes.

Despite this, Jews were allowed to live in Christian lands and to follow their own faith. There was a practical reason for this. Christians were not allowed to earn a living as money lenders, and the Jews could perform this useful role. The Church also taught that the presence of Jews was a good thing.

It reminded Christians of Christ and his death on the cross.

Ordinary Christians were suspicious of Jews and accused them of all sorts of crimes, such as poisoning wells and killing Christian children in secret religious ceremonies. Whenever a new crusade was launched against Muslims, there were anti-Jewish riots in England. People said, '*Why should we go overseas to kill God's enemies when we can do it at home?*'. The worst riot of all took place at York, on 16 March 1190. A group of 150 Jews were sheltering in the castle from a mob, which was threatening to kill them unless they became Christians. The group of Jews chose to kill themselves instead.

Life for Britain's Jews grew worse during King Edward I's reign. The king taxed them so heavily that they soon had no money left. Then, in 1290, Edward banished all Jews from his kingdom. Jews did not return to Britain until the seventeenth century.

Until the late 1300s, few Christians ever questioned the teachings of the Church. Most people accepted what their priest told them on trust. Few could read the Bible themselves since it was only available in Latin. In any case, all books were handwritten and were therefore very expensive.

John Wycliffe

The first people to question Church teaching were themselves Churchmen, people who had been able to study the Bible. In fourteenth-century England, the most important of them was a university teacher called John Wycliffe. He began by attacking the wealth of the Church and went on to disagree with many of its teachings. He said that the holy bread did not really change into Christ's body during mass.

Wycliffe believed that ordinary people should be allowed to read the Bible for themselves, and he began translating it into English. A churchman called Henry of Knighton wrote:

'In this way, the Gospel became open to laymen and badly educated women. This was like scattering pearls to be trodden underfoot by swine.'

The new ideas of the Lollards

Many Catholic teachings, such as the idea of purgatory and the power of saints, were not in the Bible. Wycliffe's followers, called 'Lollards' (mumblers), believed that all such ideas should be rejected. They said that the Catholic Church had twisted the true faith and they described the pope as *'a great beast and a devil of hell'*.

The Lollards had no respect for Church services, such as the mass. One of them, John Montague, showed what he thought of it by spitting the holy bread into his hand and taking it home to eat with his oysters.

King Henry IV and his bishops were determined to stamp out Lollard beliefs. In 1401, a law was passed stating that Lollards who refused to change their opinions would be burned. Soon after, a man called William Sawtry became the first Lollard to die at the stake. Over 100 more executions followed.

Although individual Lollards could be killed, it was impossible to stop new ideas from spreading. This was especially true once cheaper books appeared with the invention of printing, in the late 1400s.

John Foxe, a sixteenth-century writer who hated the Catholic Church, wrote:

'The pope must either abolish knowledge and printing, or printing must at length root him out (destroy him).'

While the king watches, heretics are burned alive. King Henry IV and his leading churchmen believed that this was the only way to deal with Lollards.

King Henry VIII, the founder and first head of the Church of England.

In the 1520s, there was a new quarrel between an English king and a pope. King Henry VIII was desperate to divorce his wife, but Pope Clement VII would not give his permission. After several years of failing to persuade the pope, Henry decided to make himself the head of the Church in England and to get a divorce from his own church courts.

The breaking up of the monasteries

As head of the Church, Henry saw many new ways of making money. He began by closing down the monasteries and selling off their lands. Around 9,000 monks and nuns were suddenly forced to find a new way of life in the outside world. At the same time, the shrines in the monastery churches and cathedrals were stripped of their treasures. The holy relics were burned.

Catholic worship is banned

There were even greater changes during the reign of Henry's son, the boy king Edward VI. Edward's ministers, who ruled on his behalf, were Protestants, people hostile to many Catholic beliefs. Protestants did not believe in purgatory, and said that the dead went straight to heaven or to hell. Without purgatory, many Church services, such as the saying of masses for the dead, were pointless. These, and other Catholic practices, were banned. Ordinary people were no longer allowed to pray to saints, or to creep to the cross on Good Friday.

At the same time, churches were stripped of their decorations. Today, if you visit a medieval cathedral, you can still see signs of the destruction of those years. You will see statues of saints with their heads missing, and bare walls which were once covered with paintings.

Similar religious changes were happening at the same time across northern Europe. These changes were so important that they are now seen to mark

The destruction of the shrines horrified many Christians. A sixteenth-century poem describes the ruined monastery of Walsingham, which had been a popular place for pilgrimages:

> *'Owls do shriek where the*
> *sweetest hymns*
> *Lately were sung;*
> *Toads and serpents hold their*
> *dens*
> *Where the palmers (pilgrims)*
> *did throng ...*
> *Sin is where Our Lady sat,*
> *Heaven turned is to hell.*
> *Satan sits where Our Lord did*
> *sway;*
> *Walsingham, O, farewell.'*

a whole new period of history. When the Catholic Church lost its control over Christianity in Europe, the Middle Ages themselves came to an end.

All over Britain, stained-glass windows were smashed in the sixteenth and seventeenth centuries, after King Henry VIII became king. Luckily, some windows survived. This fourteenth-century picture of God comes from Kidlington Church, in Oxfordshire.

Timeline

AD 526	St Benedict founds his first monastery at Monte Cassino in Italy
597	St Augustine begins to spread Christianity in southern England
1066	Normans conquer England
1095	First Crusade sets off to conquer the Holy Land
1098	Cistercian order of monks founded, at Citeaux in France
1120	Knights Templars founded
1128	first Cistercian monastery in Britain, at Waverly
1170	murder of Thomas Becket, archbishop of Canterbury
1190	King Richard the Lionheart sets off on the Third Crusade. Jews at York massacred
1208	King John quarrels with Pope Innocent III. The pope places an 'Interdict' on England, banning Church services
1215	Pope Innocent III decrees that all adult Christians should go to confession and communion at least once a year
1221	Dominican friars come to England
1224	Franciscan friars come to England
1290	Jews forced to leave England
1347-48	a plague called the 'Black Death' kills a third of the population of Britain
1370s	John Wycliffe criticises the teachings of the Church. His followers are called Lollards
1401	first burning of a Lollard
c1450	invention of printing, in Germany
1534	King Henry VIII becomes head of the Church of England
1536-40	closing down of the monasteries

Anchorites People who chose to be walled up alone in a small cell, called an anchorhold, for religious reasons.

Bible The Christian holy book, made up of the Old Testament, the Jewish holy books, and the New Testament, a selection of early Church writings. Christians believed that the Bible was the word of God.

Bishop A powerful churchman in charge of all the priests in an area of the country called a diocese.

Blessing Church ceremony, including a sprinkling of holy water, used to protect someone or something from the devil.

Cathedral A large church which was also the headquarters of a bishop, who had his cathedra, or throne, there.

Chancel The holiest part of a church, almost always at its eastern end. It was separated from the nave by railings (*cancelli*). The priest said mass before the altar in the chancel.

Crusades Christian holy wars, mostly fought against Muslims. There were also crusades against heretics, in the south of France.

Curse A form of words, used by a priest, asking God to punish a wicked person or an evil spirit.

Dammed People whose souls are in hell.

Excommunicated Excommunication was a punishment in which someone was forced to leave the membership of the Church so that they would be unable to benefit from any Church service. This was like being handed over to the devil. Christians believed that if someone died while excommunicated, they would go to hell.

Fasting To go without food, mainly for religious reasons.

Friars Members of a Christian brotherhood set up to spread the faith by preaching.

Heretics Christians who disagreed with the Church's official teachings. The ideas of a heretic were called 'heresy'.

Hermits People who lived alone for religious reasons. Hermits, unlike anchorites, were free to move from place to place.

Masses Church services thought to change bread and wine into the body and blood of Jesus Christ. When the bread was eaten, it was called taking communion.

Miracle An unlikely and almost impossible event that people in the Middle Ages believed was an act of God

Monks Members of a religious brotherhood living in a monastery, also known as a priory or an abbey.

Nave The public part of a church, where the ordinary people worshipped.

Nuns Members of a religious sisterhood living in a nunnery.

Order A brotherhood of monks or friars, or a sisterhood of nuns, following a particular rule or way of life.

Penances Any actions to make amends to God for sins. Penances included fasting, saying prayers or going on a pilgrimage. Lent, in the late winter, was the season of penance. Everyone fasted during Lent.

Pilgrimage A journey to a holy place, such as Jerusalem, the city where Christ died, or to the shrine of a saint.

Pope The Bishop of Rome and the head of the Catholic Church.

Priests Churchmen who looked after the religious needs of ordinary people. Only a priest had the power to say mass.

Purgatory A place of suffering, where most Christians were thought to go after death to burn away their sins. Once they had done this, they could go to heaven.

Rebels People who refuse to obey the orders given by a person in authority.

Relics Holy objects linked with Christ or a saint. Relics included bones and items of clothing. They were thought to have great powers.

Saints Holy people who had been given great powers by God. The saints in heaven could help people still living on earth.

Shrine A holy place or a container for something holy, such as the tomb of a saint or a box holding a relic.

Sins Thoughts or actions displeasing to God. There were 'seven deadly sins': anger, sloth (laziness), avarice (greed for gain), gluttony (greed for food), lust, envy and pride.

Books to read

A Medieval Cathedral by J. James (Simon and Schuster, 1991)

A Medieval Monastery by F. MacDonald and G. Wood (Simon and Schuster, 1994)

Castles and Cathedrals by D. Aldred (Cambridge University Press, 1993)

Medieval Wall Paintings by E. Clive Rouse (Shire Publications, 1991)

Places to visit
Cathedrals

The best medieval cathedrals to visit are :

Canterbury Cathedral
  Tel: (01227) 762 862

Durham Cathedral, County Durham
  Tel: (01424) 422 964,

Ely Cathedral Tel: (01353) 667 735

Exeter Cathedral Tel: (01392) 55573

Lincoln Cathedral Tel: (01522) 544 544

Norwich Cathedral Tel: (01603) 626 290

St David's Cathedral, Dyfed
  Tel: (01473) 720 202

Wells Cathedral Tel: (01749) 74483

Winchester Cathedral Tel: (01962) 53137

York Cathedral Tel: (01904) 622 774

Monasteries

Battle Abbey, Battle, Sussex
  Tel: (01424) 773 792

Fountains Abbey, Ripon, Yorkshire
  Tel: (01765) 608 888

Rievaulx Abbey, Rievaulx, Yorkshire
  Tel: (01439) 798 228

Index

Numbers in **bold** refer to illustrations within the text.